I0462204

COMING TO TERMS
WITH WALL STREET

"Look that up in your *Funk and Wagnall's*."

Rowan and Martin, 1968.

COMING TO TERMS WITH WALL STREET

AN INSIDER'S GUIDE TO INVESTMENT TERMINOLOGY

Gary B. Helms

Writer's Showcase
presented by *Writer's Digest*
San Jose New York Lincoln Shanghai

Coming to Terms with Wall Street
An Insider's Guide to Investment Terminology

All Rights Reserved © 2000 by Gary B. Helms

No part of this book may be reproduced or transmitted in any form or
by any means, graphic, electronic, or mechanical, including photocopying,
recording, taping, or by any information storage retrieval system,
without the permission in writing from the publisher.

Writer's Showcase
presented by *Writer's Digest*
an imprint of iUniverse.com, Inc.

For information address:
iUniverse.com, Inc.
5220 S 16th, Ste. 200
Lincoln, NE 68512
www.iuniverse.com

ISBN: 0-595-15506-5

Printed in the United States of America

Dedicated to the small investor…..
with the hope that, in the fullness of time,
he will become a large investor.

A

A. SULKA

Where Wall Streeters buy their shirts in up years.

ABSOLUTE RETURN STRATEGIES

Investment schemes to which the unwary are certain to return at absolutely the wrong time.

ACCOUNTANT

One who describes the horse, in excruciating detail, once it is out of the barn.

ACCRETIVE

What most mergers are alleged to be to earnings, in the first year, but rarely are.

ACTUARY

Someone lacking the personality to become an accountant.

AEROSPACE INDUSTRY

What all of American industry would be like if government and business cooperated better. (See Screwdriver, Ninety Dollars.)

AFTERGLOW

Watching the runoff after a particularly good day.

AGRICULTURE

A typically non-profit activity engaged in by farmers to produce food and fiber. Agriculture is to bullfighting, some say, as education is to football.

AIRLINE FOOD

- ❖ Cuisine typically one notch above that available at Financial Analysts Federation lunches.
- ❖ Some say, an oxymoron.

AIRLINES

A group of stocks greatly favored by Wall Street analysts, financial journalists, college professors, and others who have no intention of actually buying them. The investment thesis is that, although the industry's cumulative profit since Kitty Hawk is negative, it may turn neutral someday.

ALL AMERICAN

A securities analyst skilled in the finer points of his profession, such as convincing brokers to actually call clients with his latest insight, and keeping a straight face when explaining that management bagged him when his most recent independently derived earnings estimate proved to be too high.

ALL HAT AND NO CATTLE

Term of derogation for the guy in the pink Cadillac on a particularly busy night at the Dallas convention.

ALL OR NONE

Amount of credit that will be taken by one's broker depending on whether an investment works out (all) or it doesn't (none).

AMICABLE SETTLEMENT

Corporate (or matrimonial) proceeding which is concluded without shots being fired.

AMICUS CURAIE BRIEFS

Calvins worn by attorneys who disdain boxer shorts.

ANALYST

One particularly anal in attitude or approach.

ANNUAL MEETING

An event typically attended by retirees, Wall Street analysts, and short sellers.

ANNUAL REPORT

The analyst's major source of information about a company, such as who to contact regarding investment banking business, how big is the pension fund and who runs it, and who might be potential clients in the sale of 144 stock. The professional always reads the annual report from back to front, ignores the chairman's letter and the pictures (except in the case of lingerie manufacturing).

ANOMALY INVESTING

- ❖ The process of strip-mining the data, via computer, for tiny market inefficiencies which might provide a scant profit after costs and commissions if some other anomalist doesn't get there first
- ❖ An investment approach based on ignoring the haystacks and seeking needles.

ANTICIPATION

The act of buying on the rumor and selling on the news.

APPAREL

An industry which attempts to earn a profit buying from the Scots and selling to the Jews.

ARBITRAGE

Investment technique that makes it possible to lose money on both sides of a trade.

ARMANI, GEORGIO

Noted Italian designer and camouflage specialist, adept at making flab look like muscle.

ARM'S LENGTH

Politically correct distance at which to keep one's date until she explicitly suggests closer contact.

As Is

Exculpatory clause often affixed to used cars.

ASPEN

Quaint little ski village populated by downhill enthusiasts, nature lovers, and people who can afford $800 sweat suits.

ASSET PLAY

A company which may have sufficient sleepy assets to support heavy debt service, investment banking fees, and a profit for the LBO firm until resold to the public as a niche market opportunity.

AUDITOR

An accountant with an attitude; what John Wayne would have been had he been an accountant.

AVERAGING DOWN

Buying more of a stock when it declines below your cost in order to reduce your average cost. Presumably the ultimate success of this strategy would be to achieve an average cost approaching zero.

AVIATION AND DAY TRADING

Two professions where one rarely encounters a practitioner who is both old and bold.

B

Babe Magnet

Solvent Miami Beach widower who can see to drive after dark.

Backlog

Unfilled orders, which may serve to dampen the impact of an economic downturn, unless of course those firms which placed the orders cancel them because they, too, realize that there is a downturn. In those cases, backlogs will disappear faster than analysts can hit their speed dials.

Backwardation

A condition said to exist in the futures market when cygnets cost more than swans.

Bakers' Dozen

Thirteen.

Brokers' Dozen

Eleven.

Bakersfield

What San Francisco would be like if it were in Texas.

Bangkok

Appropriately named emerging market center and world capital of ladies ping pong.

Balanced Fund

Pool of capital with investment objectives designed in such a way that nobody is responsible to anybody, no matter what happens.

Banking

An industry founded on the concept that if your analysis is correct, and the economy holds together, you will get your money back.

Barbell

Typical portfolio construction when the bond manager doesn't know which way to go.

DUMBBELL

A bond manager who doesn't know he doesn't know.

BASKET

* ❖ Prepackaged portfolio of stocks selected to represent a market sector, industry group, etc.

* ❖ Decorative item often artfully displayed by followers of Martha Stewart.

BEAN COUNTER

* ❖ A particularly obnoxious budget director.

* ❖ Whoever approves your expense account.

* ❖ A first time diner at Taco Bell.

BEANS, THE

Soybeans, the commodity favored by sophisticated commodity traders in both New York and Chicago because of their two key characteristics: unsophisticated investors and volatility.

CRUSH, THE

What happens to unsophisticated investors in the beans.

BEAR

One skilled in finding a cloud in every silver lining.

BEAR HUG

Legislative technique utilized by the governor of Minnesota. (See Body Slam.)

BEAR MARKET

Period of time in which money reverts to its rightful owners.

BEAR MARKET LIMO

The I.R.T.

BEARISH TREND

A memo from Ace Greenberg.

BEAVIS AND BUTTHEAD

Role models for "Generation X'ers" and future bond salesmen.

BEIGE BOOK

The current aged and decrepit look of Alan Greenspan's infamous little black book from his bachelor days.

BENCHMARK

The indentation left when "Refrigerator" Perry is sent into the game.

BERKSHIRE HATHAWAY

The highest-priced stock on the New York Stock Exchange and among the least widely held. Astonishingly, it is impossible to attend a cocktail party without meeting someone who has owned it for years.

BETA

- ❖ A measure of how risky the consultant thinks your portfolio is.

- ❖ A stock's sensitivity to market direction, thought to explain 90% of a stock's move.

ALPHA

A measure of company specific factors, thought to explain 70% of a stock's move.

BLATHER

A set of arguments about stock prices constructed and used by those who never owned a stock. (See Balderdash.)

BETTING THE JOCKEY INSTEAD OF THE HORSE

The belief that clever management is more important to a company's future than the kind of business the company is in. A very different view is held by those who favor owning companies that any fool could run, because "eventually, one will."

BIG BLUE

- ❖ The International Business Machines Corporation.

- ❖ The former police car driven by the Brothers, Elwood and Jake.

- ❖ Marge Simpson's hair style.

BIG BOARD

What John Wayne used to surf on.

BILLABLE HOUR

About 12.5 minutes, on average.

"BILLIONAIRE NEXT DOOR, THE"

A book of financial advice which analyzes the methods of ordinary people in Palo Alto.

"BILLOWS ASTERN AND THREE SHEETS TO THE WIND"

Apt description of more than one former commodore of the New York Yacht Club.

BIRKENSTOCKS

Politically correct footwear, often affected by those lobbying for more computer memory.

BITING COMMENTARY

A play-by-play activity sometimes carried on by Marv Albert.

BLIND POOL

A joint venture between Ray Charles and Little Stevie Wonder.

BLIP

Meaningless piece of economic data which is contrary to what you had forecast.

ABERRATION

Two such blips in a row.

STATISTICAL TRAP

One aberration plus a blip.

BLOOD ON THE SCARECROW, TEARS ON THE PLOW

The theme of an analyst's report when he again reduces his earnings estimate for Deere and Company.

BLOW BY BLOW DESCRIPTION

What was given by the media during most of 1998-1999.

Blue Moon

Approximate frequency of occasions when specialists have actually risked their own capital on likely losing trades in order to maintain a fair and orderly market.

BMW

Machine used ultimately to drive in 35 mile per hour traffic and to the dealership for monthly tune-ups.

Bond Daddies

Municipal bond salesmen from Memphis, said to be overly fond of blue suede shoes, obscure issuers, and investment naifs.

Bonus Pool

A reward not paid until December, primarily to cover guarantees that management made in January, and about the only reason the whole Research Department doesn't walk out in April.

Book Value

A purely historical figure on the balance sheet, sometimes used by analysts as a last resort to justify an overpriced stock.

Boston

Land of the bean and the cod, of the prudent man rule and home to a number of money management firms. And, yes, it is possible to get schrod in Boston.

Bottom Fishing

An attempt to buy depressed stocks at or near their lows. Even if successful, tends to fill the portfolio with Bottom Feeders.

Bottom Line

- ❖ That which all corporate actions are supposed to impact.
- ❖ To some, the major attraction of the *Sports Illustrated* swimsuit issue.

Bottoms Up Investing

The tendency, during bull markets, to celebrate new holdings with libations at Harry's.

BOUTIQUE

A firm supplying only limited service, usually slower and at a premium fee.

THE BOYS ARE BACK IN TOWN

Morgan Stanley sponsors yet another new issue luncheon.

BRAZIL

An economy which always has had, and some say always will have, great potential.

THE BRIDGES OF MADISON AVENUE

Sappy romantic novel about the advertising business.

BROAD TAPE

The ribbon used to demark the end of the annual Wall Street Women's 10-K race.

BROADWAY

- ❖ Another street of dreams which, unlike Wall Street, is said to have a neon light for every broken heart it produced.

- ❖ A politically incorrect term meant to convey feminine proclivities, similar to dameway and chickway.

BROCHURE

Document containing numerous pictures of the firm's principals in various heroic poses. Produced in color on very slick paper and prized by consultants who file, cross reference, and sometimes read the material.

BROWSER

One who browses and is therefore not a customer.

BTU TAX AND HEALTH CARE REFORM

The two central tenets of the Clintons' economic program, the passage of either of which would have aborted the recovery and prevented a second Clinton term.

BUFFETT, WARREN

The sage of Omaha, possessed of more social skills than Bill Gates and most quoted, least emulated investor in America.

BULGE BRACKET

The key determinant, some say, to Tom Jones' long-lived popularity with the ladies.

BULL

Half of the riposte often given by investors when their broker suggests averaging down.

BULL MARKET STAGES

EARLY

When people avoid you upon learning that you are an investment professional.

LATE

When the same people ask you for tips.

VERY LATE

When they give *you* tips.

BULLISH

What it is very important to be in a bull market.

BUNS OF STEEL

What you may purchase at the Broad Street Deli on the morning after a three-day weekend.

BUSINESSMAN'S RISK

An investment idea so utterly lacking in merit that it can only appeal to the perverse nature of those psychopathically uncomfortable in the consensus. (See Contrarianism.)

BUST

What follows boom in the dictionary, not immediately but inevitably.

BUTTAFOUCO

Italian verb meaning to exhibit impatience, e.g. to drink a wine before its time.

BUYING EARLY

An investment mistake not nearly so serious as selling late.

C

CNBC

The place to get changes in your broker's firm's thinking before your broker does.

Capital Market Theory

An academic hypothesis based on the unlikely and pragmatically absurd proposition that investors act rationally. In the capital theorist's world, no one draws to inside straights, bets long shots, or buys lottery tickets, and everybody bets the favorite to show.

Capital Spending

What the guys in the Capitol do best.

Carbon-Based Life Form With No Felony Convictions

Minimum qualifications these days to get a major credit card.

Cardinal Rule of Equine Investments

"Never own anything that eats."

Carloadings

4:59 on the Erie Lackawana.

Carpe Diem

Latin phrase meaning: "Eat some fish every day."

Cash Cow

A corporate activity or asset which, like the bovine for which it is named, produces both milk and excrement, hopefully in proportions acceptable to its owner.

"Cash Is Trash"

A sentiment never known to have been uttered at, or in the vicinity of, a market bottom.

Caveat Emptor

Latin phrase meaning beware of new issues and secondary offerings.

CARPET BURN

Sports injury often sustained by a true sport.

CARVEOUT

A solution sometimes utilized by drilling partnerships and Lorena Bobbitt.

CAVIAR HELPER

Food additive used by Beverly Hills housewives during times of economic difficulty.

CELL PHONE

Device used much more often to check prices than to place orders.

CEREAL PHILANDERER

Kellogg's worst nightmare, a consumer who shows no loyalty to a particular brand of corn flakes.

CHAIRMAN OF THE BOARD

Often the CEO, and always Frank Sinatra.

CHASEN'S

Home of the best $19 bowl of chili in all of Beverly Hills.

CHAT ROOM

A place more anonymous than a singles bar in a strange town.

CHAUVINIST

One who says out loud that a crowd of men thinks like a single woman.

CHEESEBURGER IN PARADISE

A description, it is said, of Mama Cass Elliot's final meal.

CHICAGO

Frank Sinatra's kind of town: blues, broads and bean traders.

CHIEF INVESTMENT OFFICER

One who takes the credit when performance is good, and shares the blame when performance is bad.

CHINESE MONEY

Yoko Ono's IRA.

CHINESE WALL

A theoretical but palpably real barrier that was erected between John Lennon and the other three Beatles.

CHOLESTEROL

The everyday special at Wolf's Deli.

CHUM

❖   Inexpensive promotional items given away by stockbrokers at conferences and meetings.

❖   Not a good form of address for a law enforcement official of any kind.

CHUMP CHANGE

What is left of a wildly successful partnership after legal fees and general partners' participation.

CHURNING

Overtrading of a client's discretionary account, which is illegal, unless the broker says he was doing it for reasons other than to generate commissions, in which case it is perfectly legal.

CIRCUS CIRCUS

One of the few places on earth where one can shoot craps and step in elephant poop at the same time.

THE CITI NEVER SLEEPS

Possible explanation for the tired and somnolent corporate strategy which led to the demise of the leading money center bank.

CIVILIAN

One who is not in the investment business. Pension plan sponsors and consultants are *of*, but not *in*, the investment business. Members of the investment press, it has been said, are in the investment business the way Howard Cosell was in football.

CLASS ACTION

Process whereby a significant amount of money is transferred from company funds into legal fees, resulting in insignificant amounts of money going to a significant number of people, all accompanied by significant press coverage.

CLETUS THE SLACK-JAWED YOKEL

Recurring character on *The Simpsons* and Secret Service code name for the brother of each of the last two Democratic presidents.

CLIENT

An especially nice fellow, possessed of wit, charm, good taste and forbearance.

PROSPECT

Same as above, but with elan.

FORMER CLIENT

An insufferable lout.

CLIENT CONFERENCE

Something that should be held every six months regardless of performance. (See Dental Appointments.) Topics of interest would include the client's golf score, the state of his business, and the economic outlook (unless of course, performance has been satisfactory).

CLOSED END FUND

A mutual fund thought to be particularly appropriate for anal retentives.

CLOUD NINE

Tina Turner and Elle MacPherson at the same time. (See Ultimate Menage.)

CLUB, THE

> *COUNTRY,* to the analyst.
>
> *YACHT,* to the portfolio manager.
>
> *GENTLEMEN'S,* to the trader.

COAST, THE

> *LOS ANGELES,* to the analyst.
>
> *SAN FRANCISCO,* to the portfolio manager.
>
> *LAS VEGAS,* to the trader.

CODE OF THE WEST

❖ Lines of software written by Bill Gates' programmers in Seattle.

❖ "There is no intelligent life east of Sepulveda."

COGNOSCENTI

People from Kansas who have been to both a state fair and a tractor pull.

COLOR COMMENTARY

Remarks made regarding the suspenders on display in the Salomon Brothers' trading room.

COMBOVER

Hairstyle affected by some investment bankers who have been known to recommend a corporate version of it to their clients, in which case it is called a "restructuring."

COMPETITION

The governing force that makes capitalism work, greatly to be desired throughout the economic system, except as applied to companies in your portfolio.

CONCENTRATION

A camp to which portfolio managers of undiversified mutual funds should be sent.

CONNECTICUT

A land of stone fences, Range Rovers, and expensive M and A lawyers.

CONSERVATIVE ESTIMATE

What the company will earn if the economy booms, everything goes right and they discover oil in the parking lot.

CONSULTANT

A guy who knows 306 ways to make love but doesn't know any girls.

CONTRARIAN

A trend follower who didn't sell in time.

CONTRARY INDICATOR

A person or publication so consistently wrong that it is profitable to act exactly opposite to the advice offered. Usually reliable contrary indicators are certain magazine covers, brokerage best-buy lists, and committee picks generally.

LEXICOGRAPHER'S NOTE:

> Random walkers, who believe in a bell curve world, are chagrined to admit that there are more contrary indicators than there are good stock pickers.

CONTROLLER OF THE CURRENCY

George Soros, according to some.

CONVENTIONAL WISDOM

That body of knowledge which stands one in good stead when attending conventions, e.g. which hospitality suites are best. (Hint: It is usually not the research firms.)

CONVERTIBLE

A security possessing the upside potential of the bond, while maintaining the safety features of the underlying stock.

CONVEXITY

A shape often assumed by middle-aged bond traders.

CORE HOLDING

A stock for which earnings estimates are neither possible nor necessary.

CORE RATE

What the inflation rate would be if it weren't for food, clothing, and shelter.

CORNER OF WALL AND BROAD

The financial center of the universe prior to the advent of the Internet.

COSELL, HOWARD

The Dan Dorfman of sports columnists.

COSMETICS

An industry based on the observable phenomenon that those old enough to afford the product need it most.

CORNER

That portion of the building where the boss's office is.

COUNTRY FUND

A mutual fund heavily invested in shares of Gaylord Entertainment and Cracker Barrell.

CRAMDOWN PREFERRED

The most popular offering in the partners' dining room.

CRICK

The sound one hears when turning on a Sony appliance.

CROSS OF GOLD SPEECH

Oration delivered by William Jennings Bryan in the 1920's to denounce the tendency, even then, for floor brokers to wear shiny amulets around their necks.

CROUPIER

One who makes money regardless of whether the little silver ball lands on red or black. Croupiers first met under a buttonwood tree in downtown Manhattan to establish and protect that right.

CRUISE

(NOUN)

Mode of travel favored by the newly wed and the nearly dead.

(VERB)

To seek out available members of the opposite sex for casual physical encounters.

CRUISE CONTROL

The VIRIS.

CRUSTY, SOMEWHAT CHEESY AND REDOLENT OF WHITE WINE

Apt description of the headwaiter at Le Cirque.

CUSTODIAN

One who performs menial and sometimes degrading tasks for a very low fee.

CUSTODIAN BANK

(See above.)

CUSTOMER POKER (GOLF, FISHING, ETC.)

The ability to insure that your client beats you just enough to exult but not enough to lose respect. Said to be particularly favored by municipal underwriters.

CUSTOMERS' MAN

The man who explains to the customers why the analyst who liked a stock at 140 calls it a weak hold at 74.

CUSTOMERS' YACHTS

Vessels typically shorter, narrower, and berthed at less expensive dockage than any broker's yacht, if indeed they exist at all.

CYBERSPACE

Yet another area rapidly becoming overstored.

CYCLICAL

A growth stock that stopped growing.

D

Da' Bears

❖ A mediocre team that plays to capacity crowds in a miserable stadium.

❖ Da' people for whom da' glass is always half full and da' news is always getting worse.

Day Job

What the day trader should not give up.

Day Trader

With some aptitude and diligence, one who can produce a good living for his discount broker and provider of chart services.

Dead On Arrival

❖ Said of bills having no chance of passage, such as those favored by Tipper Gore to censor rock lyrics.

❖ Jerry Garcia and friends when the tour bus enters the stadium.

Debutante

One who doesn't engage in group sex because she'd have to write all those thank you notes.

December Silver

What is sometimes exchanged by the wife for January platinum.

Decedent

Said to be the only participant in an Irish wake not inebriated.

Defensive Stock

An oxymoron, like military intelligence or ladies field hockey.

Delayed Arrival

Commutation via the Long Island Railroad.

DENVER

Investment center of the Rocky Mountain region, Mecca to drilling fund promoters, and a place where you can become a member of the Mile High Club in the privacy of your hotel room.

DERIVATIVES

Synthetic securities from which brokers *derive* a significant portion of their income.

DESTINATION RESORT

A facility sufficiently luxurious to be able to locate far enough off the beaten path so as to enjoy monopoly pricing power for basic necessities.

DIET COLA, ASSERTIVENESS TRAINING, AND EARLY MASS

Three things most utilized by those least in need of them.

DIFFERENT STROKES

What you will see a lot of at the annual Salomon Brothers golf tournament.

DILUTION

Something almost always evident in the cocktails at an airport bar.

DISCO

A music substitute popular in the 70's characterized primarily by the costumes worn by its enthusiasts. Current version is called hip-hop.

DISCOUNT BROKER

A securities dealer who admits that he provides no service beyond bare execution.

DISCRETIONARY ACCOUNT

A repository for the firm's less successful offerings, particularly those with good long-term prospects and large selling concessions.

DISPOSABLE INCOME

That which is available after the kids leave home and the dog dies.

D.K.

"Don't kare," a shorthand denial that the broker knows about or cares about the trade in question.

DNA Evidence

Proof so powerful that it takes really expensive lawyers and an irresponsible jury to overcome it.

Dog

❖　An underperformer in a portfolio.

❖　A low priced stock (cats and dogs).

❖　A female security analyst.

❖　The team not favored.

Dog Eat Dog

The Bengals play the Falcons.

Door-to-Door

Intimate conversations between Jim Morrison and other members of the Band from Venice.

Double Header

Two successive (and successful) romantic encounters in the same evening.

Triple Header

Although quite common in the 50's, 60's, 70's and early 80's, not known to occur since.

Down and Out

A courtship technique allegedly utilized on Paula Jones.

Down Round

An unmitigated coup in venture capital whereby the original investor in a disastrous enterprise is able to lay off a portion of his loss to a new investor enticed by a lower price.

Drug Dealer

One whose gross margins approach those of a private money manager.

Dry Hole

One of several reasons that an oil well, or for that matter a relationship, might be deemed unsuccessful.

Dude

NASDAQ trader with a pierced body part.

Dunkin' Donuts

What many police officers are doin' by the time their shift is an hour old.

Durable Goods

Products typically produced in West Germany or Japan.

Duration

A measure of how long a bond trader *endures* in an average romantic encounter. It is determined by a complicated formula, but is said not to be very long.

Dutch Auction

What is sometimes conducted in the red light district of Amsterdam.

E

E. Coli

Hopefully, not an adjunct to two all beef patties, special sauce and pickle on a sesame seed bun.

Early Withdrawal Penalty

Redress exacted for premature completion of a social engagement. In extreme cases, may occasion denial of the right to make future entries.

EBITDA

❖ Everything Bumped Into Debt Amortization
 A rough measure of just how leveraged this puppy is.

❖ Expect Big Interest To Delay Appreciation
 Since there will be no earnings anytime soon, analysts (who, after all, have to compute something), compute what earnings would have been without debt service, taxes, depreciation and cost of goods sold. Kind of like what your golf score would be like assuming no traps, rough or hazards, and a big funnel in front of the cup.

Economics

What economists do. (See Economist.)

Economist

One who studies or practices economics.

Edinburgh

Home of canny Scotch investors, unfair golf courses, and very strange breakfast meats.

Efficient Frontier

Hypothetical limit beyond which it does not make economic sense for the modern portfolio theorist to design or market "product;" the point at which the client's eyes glaze over.

Efficient Market Theory

An academic hypothesis which asserts that U.S. Surgical was properly priced at 130 and also at 16.

"Eight Dollars a Trade"

A very small fraction of what a bad execution can cost you.

Electable

Said of a charismatic politician with a short arrest record.

Elasticity

Important characteristic of Mama Cass Elliot's gym shorts.

Elliot Wave

Undulating motion created by Elliot and other fans at sports events and rock concerts. (See "Tastes Great—Less Filling" routine.)

E-mail

Modern mode of communication combining the simplicity of cuneform with the privacy of smoke signals.

Engine Charlie Wilson

The last CEO of General Motors to increase market share.

Engineering

The corporate department which, given enough time, can make an original design uglier, clumsier, and more expensive to produce.

Enhanced Memory

What every wife has with regard to any of her husband's lapses. This attribute does not seem to apply to where she parked at the mall or whether she made entries in your joint checkbook.

Euro

A new currency combining the dynamism of the Deustche Mark with the stability of the Peseta.

Ex

Without, as ex-dividend, which is a stock trading without the recently declared dividend. Excreta is something said to be what comes out of the Research Department.

EXCULPATORY CLAUSE

The place at the bottom of research reports when it says, "Don't blame us if this thing blows up in your face."

EXIT STRATEGY

The act of making holiday airplane reservations early.

EXOGENOUS VARIABLE

From "outside the system," i.e. a variable not in the econometrician's computer model. Examples are consumer preferences, buyer's strikes, style changes, and other everyday and normal determinants of economic activity.

EXPENSIVE BUSINESS MEAL

A hotdog with fries at any major airport.

EXPLORATORY WELL

Good way to reduce the value of an oil property in case it comes up dry.

EXTRACTIVE INDUSTRY

An enterprise typically characterized by high costs and low profits, except in the case of dentistry.

EXTRAPOLATION

Method of forecasting which assumes that recent trends will continue at the same rate. Many extrapolators now believe that, in twenty years, two in five Americans will be Elvis impersonators.

EXTREME SPORTS

Bond traders out on the town, typically recognizable by extensive use of gold chains, pinkie rings, and bizarre color combinations.

EXTROVERTED COMPUTER NERD

One who looks at *your* shoes when talking to you.

F

Fair Value

When both cash and futures indicate a market direction that the commentator has forecast.

Fannie May—Houston

Planned re-make of the hit movie *Debbie Does Dallas*.

Fast Food

What you could get at McDonald's when Ray Kroc was alive.

Fast Track

The exit often made by philandering portfolio managers at the slightest hint of discovery. (See Risk Aversion.)

Fax

A machine that has revolutionized the way the secretarial pool orders lunch.

February

The month in which, historically, the fewest bad investment decisions are made.

Fed

What some economists hope to be as a result of analyzing monetary phenomena.

A Few Good Men

That which is desperately needed by the many widows in Miami Beach nursing homes.

Fidelity

A place where the magazines in the lobby are older than the fund managers, and you can check your fund balance at midnight on a Saturday.

Fifty-fifty Bets

Propositions that, on a fair wheel, you will lose about 60% of the time.

Financial Ratios

Several relationships that are crucial to investment success:

CURRENT RATIO

That percentage of a brokerage firm's recommended list that its research department actually likes *currently*: 20% or above is considered unusual.

ACID TEST RATIO

The percentage of stocks on the brokerage firm's list that its analysts actually own. This number is often so low as to be useless.

PAYOUT RATIO

The percentage of commissions which the firm pays out to the institutional salesman.

QUICK RATIO

The speed with which the salesman reacts to a change in his payout.

FINANCIAL SUPERMARKET

A firm so widely diversified in several financial services that it will do a mediocre job, and make very little money, in each.

FINE TUNING

The process whereby an analyst reduces his earnings estimate while maintaining a "buy" rating. (There is no comparable term for situations where an analyst raises his estimate, since such instances are so rare.)

FIRST CALL

Computerized system of disseminating research which helps analysts avoid embarrassment by having earnings estimates that are outside the consensus.

"FIRST DO NO HARM"

What should be the motto for financial planners.

FIRST RULE OF MONEY MANAGEMENT

"Don't Lose Money." The second rule of money management is "Don't Forget the First Rule."

FISCAL POLICY

One of the two major methods for the central government to damage a good economy.

FIVE AND TEN, NOW AND THEN

Typical bid and ask for a Bulletin Board issue, along with trading frequency.

FIVE HUNDRED, THE

- ❖ An index compiled by Standard and Poor's which is the most widely used method to embarrass portfolio managers.
- ❖ Reportedly, the daily caloric intake of Calista Flockhart.

FIVE STAR RATING

Grade achieved, seemingly, in some time period or for some category, by every mutual fund in America. Often those that didn't make it were merged into those that did.

FLIGHT TO QUALITY

- ❖ Financial version of foxhole religion, whereby investors worried about market weakness sell their questionable holdings at depressed prices and bid up shamelessly for perceived quality, almost always too late.
- ❖ A plane ticket to Caneel Bay.

FLOAT

(NOUN)

The number of shares that float or trade freely.

(VERB)

To negotiate or arrange a loan.

- ❖ What may happen to the body of the borrower who fails to repay Big Julie in a timely way.

FLOATER

- ❖ An investment medium first popularized by Nathan Detroit.
- ❖ A non-sinker.

FLOWER BOND

Bloomin' debenture that, like a cactus, blooms once.

FORCE MAJEURE

A fortuitous event which allows the abrogation of ill-conceived contracts.

FOREIGN AID

The practice of taking money from the poor in rich countries and giving to the rich in poor countries.

FOREPLAY

Preliminary activity in Wall Street of very short duration. (See New York Minute and Nanosecond.)

40 AND OUT

The combined ages of Jerry Lee Lewis' first three wives when they moved "out."

FORTY-TWO FEET LONG AND SLEEPS SIX

The conference table at Morgan Stanley headquarters.

FREE LUNCH

A Wall Street tradition, but recommended only for those well able to afford it. Thought to be almost as expensive as free love.

FTSE ("FOOTSIE")

What one sometimes plays with comely British lasses at staid dinner parties. Often applied to other covert activity where the ultimate objective is the same.

FOSSIL FUEL

Slang term for the cuisine served in the partners' dining room at Lazard Freres.

FRACTAL GEOMETRY AND CHAOS THEORY

Yet another attempt by the academic community to quantify fear and greed.

FULL CAMBRIDGE

Chinos, leather elbow patches, and a beard but no mustache.

FULL CLEVELAND

A mode of dress comprised of a plaid jacket, bright solid trousers, and matching white patent leather belt and loafers.

MODIFIED CLEVELAND

As above, with color combination reversed.

CLEVELAND SPORT

One dressed as above, with a mustache and bow tie.

FUTURES AND OPTIONS

Two ways to hedge against capital gains.

G

G Spot

A theoretical area said to be the spot price below which gold will not trade. Discovered by a male physician, its existence is doubted by many.

GAAP

All too often, grudgingly accepted accounting principles. (See forensic accounting.)

Gaffers, Grips, and Groupies

Craft people who supply the basic services for making a motion picture and the reason, some say, that it's so expensive to shoot in Hollywood.

Geezer

Someone five years older than you.

Whippersnapper

Someone five years younger than you.

Geo Metro

A mode of transportation available at off-airport rental agencies in emergencies. It has a higher top speed but somewhat slower acceleration than a pair of in-line skates.

Geographically Undesirable

- ❖ Strong companies in unstable countries.
- ❖ Girls from Staten Island.

Ghetto Triathlon

A mugging, a holdup, and a drive-by shooting.

Glass Ceiling

Construction feature at Corning, where they also have glass floors and glass walls.

Gnarly

Description of a big up-volume day on the Pacific Coast Stock Exchange.

Golden Rule

Whoever has the gold makes the rules.

Going Public

An alternative, for some high tech companies, to going broke.

Good Vibrations

❖ What some New Age security analysts claim they can sense in a stock about ready to move up in price.

❖ A hand-held appliance sometimes stowed in the luggage of female analysts.

"Goodbye, Mr. Chips"

What you might as well say upon entering the main casino at Caesar's.

Goodwill

An item that should be carried on the balance sheet at $1.

Graduate School of Business at the University of Chicago

An institution whose graduates believe that if you can't count it, it didn't happen.

Graham, Benjamin

The father of security analysis, and author of the best selling, least read book since Dostoevski.

Gravy

Along with beer and Tabasco Sauce, the three basic food groups of Texas.

Green

❖ Meant to typify those actions, activities, and investments which help to preserve nature's precious ecology.

❖ The color a plant manager turns when presented EPA requirements to preserve the ecology.

Green Shoe

❖ An over-allotment of a new issue which can be taken down at the discretion of the investment banker.

❖ One of several thousand shades of footwear said to be included in Ms. Marcos' collection.

Greenspan, Alan

Noted inflation hawk and proponent of the preemptive strike. Is said to don condom before ringing doorbell.

Gresham's Law

"Bad money drives out good," which can be extended to other financial instruments, such as IPO's.

Gridlock

An electronic device on the cable box which prevents overindulgence in watching pro football….. a "v" chip for adult males.

Gross Margin

The obscene amount of money made by Goldman partners in good years.

Gross National Product

That portion of total economic activity involving gross (lewd, lascivious, or disgusting) activity. Thought to be gaining as a percentage of total national product.

Ground Control to Major Tong

The way the Queens office of Paine Webber signs on the squawk box for the morning call.

Growth Investing

The art of buying tadpoles and selling frogs.

Gucci

An Italian designer of small gold horseshoes and stirrups, often affixed to footwear and/or bond traders.

Guilts

Nagging feelings of remorse one may feel after sampling the nightlife of London.

Gun Control Laws

The first step in ascertaining that a high percentage of certified public accountants will turn in their hand guns.

GUNSLINGER

A term of derogation in bear markets, adulation in bull markets, and almost always applied to a portfolio manager with a faster reaction time and a better broker call than you.

GUST LARYNGITIS

The minor throat condition thought to be caused by oral contact with Gennifer Flowers.

H

Hamptons, The

A place where Manhattanites can escape Manhattan with other Manhattanites and live as they did in Manhattan.

Hands-on Experience

A practice highly advocated by former Surgeon General Joycelyn Elders.

Harley

Porcine form of transportation utilized by some bond traders on weekends. While very fuel efficient, it seems to require a temporary tattoo and screw-on earring.

Hartford

Capital city of Connecticut and home of the buy and hold strategy.

Harvard

- ❖ Eastern school of higher learning which reportedly produces a man you can always tell, but you can't tell very much.

- ❖ Home of the Business School, whose case method has indisputably done more to enable graduates to talk a good game than any other.

Headhunters

The Arkansas Highway Patrol, reportedly.

Hedge Fund

An investment partnership which derives its name from the observation that the limited partners are often "clipped" or "trimmed."

"Here's Looking At You, Kid"

Typical toast proposed to the youthful portfolio managers at Fidelity.

Highly Confident

What one can be that Mr. Millkin will again appear in the investment business.

HIPPOCRATIC OATH

An ancient code of conduct for the medical profession, often displayed in doctors' offices. It begins, "Fees are due and payable when service is rendered."

HIRING FREEZE

A management technique usually followed by a hiring panic, thereby ensuring the prosperity of management recruiters everywhere.

HOG HEAVEN

The pork belly pit at the Merc.

HOLD

A sale. In Wall Street usage, stocks recommended for purchase are called "buys," stocks which should be sold are called "holds," and "sales" are stocks which the firm does not follow.

HOLLYWOOD

❖   A type of gin rummy wherein three games are played at once, not unlike a complicated futures strategy.

❖   A town, according to the late Fred Allen, where all the available sincerity could be contained in a flea's navel, with room left over for three caraway seeds and an agent's heart.

HONEST POLITICIAN

One who, as they say, when bought stays bought.

HONORE DE BALZAC

Fractured French expression used in Wall Street to mean "no hitting below the belt."

HOSTILE OFFER

When a New York waitress asks if you'd like more coffee.

HOT HAND

❖   Any portfolio manager who has beaten the S&P 500 in the prior quarter.

❖   Nathan Portnoy, in his younger years.

HOT ISSUE

A new offering unavailable to you or anybody you like.

Hot Walker

❖ A race track employee responsible for walking a thoroughbred after workouts to prevent it from cooling down too fast.

❖ An analyst assigned to write reports on the firm's successful underwritings which are clearly too high to be bought.

Hothouse Plant

A portfolio manager unable to interact effectively with clients or other outsiders.

Houston

The first word ever received from space, and the last word in big hair.

I

Ideal Product, The

A product you can make for a dime, sell for a dollar, and it is habit forming. Examples are cigarettes, crack cocaine, and perfume.

Illigittimi non Carbordundum

Official motto of institution brokers everywhere…..from the Latin "Don't let the bastards grind you down."

Illumination

The observed phenomenon that blondes have more fun, perhaps because they're easier to find in the dark.

Immortal Lock

- ❖ A seven high straight in five card stud when the best hand showing is AAKJ.
- ❖ Schlage.
- ❖ Shorting an institutional favorite when it closes unched after issuance of an 80-page buy report.

Inappropriate Relationship

The receipt of sexual favors by a married CEO from a low-level employee on Company time in Company facilities during normal working hours, resulting in false denials. Some stoutly maintain it should be his own private business.

Income Stock

A stock whose prospects are so bad that its price has dropped to a level where its yield is high until the dividend is cut.

Incurable Romantic

One who has contracted both herpes and AIDS.

Index Fund

A pool of capital *guaranteed* to underperform its target index, by the amount of fees and trading commissions. The concept has been improved with "tilt" funds which can be designed to underperform other, more sophisticated indices. It is believed that there are vehicles currently in the design stage that will be able to underperform *all* indices.

INDIANAPOLIS

A natural home for those too dumb for New York City and too ugly for L.A.

INFORMATION HIGHWAY

Partially paved gravel road with potholes, speed traps, and detours inexplicably favored by Wall Street commuters.

INNUENDO

An Italian suppository.

INSIDE INFORMATION

A way to lose money illegally.

INSTANT GRATIFICATION

Sense of satisfaction that takes, by Wall Street standards, too long.

INSTITUTIONAL SALESMAN

A person with a good personality, a fresh shoeshine, and accounts that are currently inactive.

INSTITUTIONAL TRADER

One who is supposed to buy two million shares of a stock that the analyst recommended at 38 and the portfolio manager authorized at 46 at a price of 54 or better when the last sale was 59 and a half.

INTELLIGENTSIA

Those bond traders whose homes contain books not requiring the use of crayons.

INTEREST RATE SENSITIVE

Any one of those issues trading on the New York, AMEX, or NASDAQ Exchanges.

INVENTORY

- ❖ Stocks or bonds that a broker-dealer currently is long in its trading account.
- ❖ Stocks or bonds that a broker-dealer currently considers very attractive for purchase.

❖   Stock that the block positioner is recommending.

INVESTMENT

A speculation that did not work out.

INVESTMENT ADVICE

GOOD

❖   Never play poker with a man called Doc or own any thing   you can't spell.

❖   Never take a job east of your degree.

PRETTY GOOD

❖   Never own anything you can't explain to a maiden aunt in five minutes.
❖   Never average down.

BAD

❖   It's already down 70%. How much lower can it go?

❖   All puts break toward the ocean.

INVESTMENT BANKER

Someone whose Research Department publishes particularly cheerful and sanguine reports.

INVESTMENT MANAGEMENT SUBSIDIARY

Device whereby the trust department is "spun off" so the chief investment officer can be paid as much as a regional loan officer.

INVESTMENT STYLE

The all-important choice of wardrobe for client conferences, and the photograph in the brochure. Choice of clothing should be consistent with the firm's geographic location and professed approach to the market. Examples of effective styles include:

NEW YORK BOUTIQUE

Armani suit with heavily moussed, straight back hair.

WEST COAST GROWTH FIRM

Shirt open three buttons down, baggy chinos, sun-bleached hair.

SOUTHWESTERN EMERGING GROWTH SHOP

Bolo tie, modified cowboy boots, suede vest.

(Mild cross-dressing is now considered allowable for private partnerships from San Francisco.)

INVESTOR RELATIONS OFFICER

The guy whose job it is to tell investors that everything is all right, and then to tell them why it wasn't.

IPO

The first chance for the lenders to bail out and the underwriters to earn a fee.

IRON RULE OF CLIENT RELATIONS, THE

"A portfolio manager without a portfolio to manage is not a portfolio manager at all."

"IT'LL BURN OFF BY NOON"

- ❖ Selling flurry of typically short duration often occurring on Monday morning after a particularly bearish forecast in *Barron's* or *Business Week*.

- ❖ Weather forecast for LaCosta, Caneel Bay, or other pricey resorts noted for perpetual sunshine.

IVY LEAGUE, THE

Grossly overpriced institutions which can nevertheless supply room, board, gym privileges, and a pretty decent education for about what it costs the City of New York to house and feed a homeless person.

J

Jackson Hole

The town, one presumes, after which Courtney Love's all-girl band was named.

Jeans Splicing

Emergency repair sometimes used by bond traders on their first visit to the country in the spring.

Jersey

- ❖ Formerly, EXXON.
- ❖ That brown smelly area visible from the twin towers on a clear day.
- ❖ Joe Wolcott's first name.

Jocular

Of or like an athlete-athletic.

Joint Venture

- ❖ An investment in a cocktail lounge, saloon, or chiropractic practice.
- ❖ Agricultural enterprise featuring Humboldt Hemp.

Junk Bond

A debenture whose rating has already been lowered.

Just-In Time Inventory

A system which provides for daily re-stocking of the senior partners' liquor cabinet.

K

Kama Sutra

A kind of instruction book for position traders.

Kansas City

Home to two mutual fund families and a place where everything is up to date, with the possible exception of storm sewers and tornado warnings.

Keel Design, Hull Speed, and Money Supply

Three subjects often discussed loudly, but not necessarily lucidly, by members of the New York Yacht Club.

Kennedy Curse, The

"Goddammit, woman, don't tell me I don't need another drink."

Keynes, John Maynard (1883-1946)

The last economist actually known to have invested successfully in the stock market.

Keynesian Economics

Theory that economic stability can be achieved by an increase in government spending during downturns and a decrease in spending during economic expansion. Unfortunately, the theory has yet to be tested, because there has never been a decrease in government spending.

"Know Your Customer" Rule

Knowledge that helps the broker overcome sales resistance when the client pleads penury upon being offered the firm's latest underwriting.

Kondratieff, Nicholai

An obscure Russian economist whose 50-year and 80-year cycles are so arcane they allow market forecasters a way to buttress any argument.

Krugerrand

A coin good for thirty minutes in Beverly Hills parking meters.

L

LaCosta

Where Los Angelenos go to overeat, overdrink, and get fit.

Laptop

❖ A portable version of the personal computer, which allows one to make questionable trades even when out of the office.

❖ A very popular dance at the Spartacus Gentlemen's Club.

LBO

A form of reorganization whereby torpid managements of tired companies are able to get a large premium for their holdings. Said to stand for "let's bail out."

Lawyerly, Reasonably Coherent, But Tedious

A pretty good description of the senior partnership at Skadden Arps.

Ledgerdemain

A performance measurement technique which elevates a portfolio's return from fourth to first quartile by careful selection of start and end points.

Lexicographers' note:

Not to be confused with Chicanery, which accomplishes the same result by selecting the right benchmark.

Legal List

Group of attorneys in downtown Manhattan who specialize in arbitration.

Lemming

The animal world's version of a momentum trader.

Lepidopterist

Most effective, and probably most profitable, user of the Net.

LEVERAGE

What you have when the clients like you better than your firm. Seriously negative leverage exists when they dislike you equally.

LIES, DAMN LIES, AND STATISTICS

Three methods used by security analysts to justify the lofty price of their favorite stock.

LIGHT, SWEET, CRUDE

Three words sometimes used to describe slightly effeminate petroleum traders on the Merc.

LIMIT DOWN

What happens when you're long.

LIMIT UP

What happens when you're short.

LIQUIDITY

A measure of the amount of alcohol consumed at investment company Christmas parties. Contrary to popular belief, liquidity is as high in bad years as good, although the quality varies.

LITIGIOUS

- ❖ A person who, when the gym is almost empty, walks up to your machine and asks politely if you're going to be long.
- ❖ Often, a person who does not now, nor does ever intend to, own a dog.
- ❖ Typically, a person who complains about foot faults in a social match.
- ❖ Anyone who has read the by-laws of the condo association.

LITTLE BLUE BOX FROM TIFFANY'S

A gift that makes a statement, "I have more money than taste. I didn't have time to shop and have no idea what you'd like. Here's a useless something that's too expensive to throw away that you probably won't hate."

LITTLE ROCK

Financial capital of central Arkansas. Cultural forebears include Pa Kettle, Jed Clampett, and Pappy Yokum.

A Little Tightening to Avoid Problems Later On

A preemptive facelift or tummy tuck.

Loaded Laggard

- ❖ A company with a depressed stock price and sufficient cash in the treasury to pay substantial legal and investment banking fees.
- ❖ The last guy to leave the office Christmas party.

Local Knowledge

The in-depth information often possessed by small regional brokers regarding local golf courses.

Locution, Locution, Locution

About the only three things the real estate manager has left to explain away poor performance in the 90's.

Lompoc, California

Site of noted rehabilitation center for arbitrageurs, high yield specialists, and other felons.

Long

- ❖ To own a position in a stock, bond, or commodity, etc.
- ❖ Harry Reems.

Long Island Expressway

- ❖ A misnomer.
- ❖ Thoroughfare populated by people who should be on the Long Island Railroad.

Long Island Railroad

A form of transportation so slow, uncomfortable, and undependable that it increases traffic on the Long Island Expressway.

Long Island Iced Tea

Sedative invented for people who commute on the Long Island Expressway or the Long Island Railroad.

LOS ANGELES

From the Spanish, "City of Lost Angels." Home to Capital Guardian, TCW, and Venice Beach. Is to family values as Miami is to alpine skiing.

LOSER'S GAME, THE

Home team fans at Wrigley Field.

LOUISIANA PURCHASE

If you're smart, the crawfish etouffe.

LOWBALL BID

An indication of willingness to buy by a broker from Nomura Securities.

LUCK

❖ What you had to overcome to produce your five-year record.

❖ That to which your competition owes his five-year record.

M

M and A

The original title for a song in *The Chorus Line*, later changed to T and A. Not to be confused with S and M, which means Sales and Marketing.

Magellan

The world's largest mutual fund, known primarily as a temporary place of employment for portfolio managers.

Making Money the Old Fashioned Way

Charging the full service rate.

Malthusian Economics

Top down rationale for buying agricultural stocks.

Mark Twain On Media Relations

"Be careful what you say to people who buy their ink by the barrel."

Market Neutral Fund

A portfolio so constructed that it can lose money regardless of market direction.

Market Timer

A person who once bought near the low or sold near the high.

Marketing

❖ What a money management firm gets very interested in when performance begins to flag.

❖ The corporate department in charge of cosmetology.

Marriage Counselor

A professional, who like the financial consultant, is unlikely to do much harm unless taken seriously.

Marriage Made in Heaven

Often said of a merger between two firms unlikely to be able to produce significant underwriting or legal fees on their own.

MARTHA'S VINEYARD

A place favored for late-night swimming by some high-spirited Washingtonians.

MATCH THE HATCH

A technique of using bait which closely resembles that which is occurring naturally on a trout stream or in the stock market, e.g. May flies, Internet retailers.

MATURITY

What a bond eventually achieves, but a bond trader often does not.

MBA

A person who never met a payroll but knows five different ways to graph one.

HARVARD MBA

A person who never met a payroll, but if he needed to, would immediately call the Payroll Department.

MEMORY

What computer people and the Clinton Administration seem never to have enough of.

MERGER OF EQUALS

Euphemism often utilized to keep key people in the acquired company from jumping ship. True mergers of equals have rarely occurred, and are disasters when they do.

METEOROLOGIST

A peculiar kind of forecaster who occasionally admits when he's wrong. There is no record of a meteorologist ever making it to Wall Street.

METRIC TON

The combined weight of Mama Cass Elliot, Sally Struthers, Meatloaf, and the Blues Brothers.

MEZZANINE FINANCING

The surreptitious balancing of the books by two brokers jointly entertaining the same client at the theater.

MID CAP

Often a stock on its way to being a large cap or a small cap.

MILLIONAIRES

People in Wall Street who were previously multi-millionaires.

MINI-MILL

Steel producer dependent on neither iron ore nor the United Steel Workers, but whose major advantage is that it gets to compete with Big Steel.

MINNEAPOLIS

Home of IDS, Mary Tyler Moore re-runs, and where people from Buffalo go for the climate.

MISSION STATEMENT

If absolutely necessary to have one, should be kept simple like that of the great Willie Mays: "When they throw it, I hit it. And when they hit it, I catch it."

MISSISSIPPI

21st state of the Union, and the main reason Arkansas is not last in education and per capita income.

"MISTAKES WERE MADE"

Self-evident but totally inadequate explanation of fourth quartile performance.

MODERN PORTFOLIO THEORY

A kind of Blackwood convention of money management, in that it allows non-money managers to talk about money management to other non-money managers.

MODERN PORTFOLIO THEORIST

One sometimes concerned that even if something works in practice, we can't be certain that it will work in theory.

MOMENTUM PLAYER

One who buys his straw hats in August.

Money Center Banks

Those financial institutions that believe money to be the center of the universe. They are distinguished from regional banks, which believe money to be the center of all creation.

Money Supply

An area of great concern for the Federal Reserve, bond traders, and economists, who cannot agree on how to measure it, how the leads and lags work, or what effect velocity has. There is unanimity, however, that it is of critical import and is currently growing either too fast or too slowly.

Mont Blanc

A decorative object d'art appearing in the shirt pocket of investment bankers. Almost always in the shape of a fountain pen, it is rarely used as such.

Monte Carlo Simulation

Artist's rendering of the late Grace Kelly.

Montezuma's Revenge

What befell people who were short Telmex.

Moore's Law

The number of analysts following a hot technology stock will *double* every eighteen months, while the quality of their collective effort will be cut in half.

Moral Suasion

One of the tools available to the Federal Reserve to control an overheating economy. It is similar in approach and effectiveness to Nancy Reagan's "Just Say No" drug initiative.

Morner

A nooner, only sooner.

Most Important Thing A Salesman Can Say

"Press firmly, you are making three copies."

Mr. Know-it-all

❖ Anyone editing your first draft or commenting on your golf swing.

❖ Anyone reviewing your purchase-and-sales report.

❖ Your second wife's first husband.

MOTION PICTURE METROPLEX

A clever means of assembling a captive audience in order to sell it a dime's worth of popcorn for $4.

N

NAFTA

An acronym meaning "Nobody Actually Free Trades Anyway" is designed to make U.S.-Mexican trade work as well elsewhere as it does within ten miles of the border.

NAKED OPTION

- ❖ An unhedged put or call position.
- ❖ Sharon Stone's occasional underwear choice.

NEANDERTHAL

A person with neither a fax machine nor a personal trainer.

NEGATIVE CARRY

When the corn costs more than you can get for the eggs.

NEPOTISM

When the senior partner's nephew works in the mailroom every summer. When you bring in your own cousin as a staff assistant, it is merely a way of reducing hiring costs.

NET

Something which very few participants on the World Wide Web are producing.

"NET" TRADE

Transaction in which you pay no commission, but allow the broker a 10% spread between bid and asked. (You have fallen into the "net.")

NEW HIGHS

What some traders on the bond desk were fervently seeking during the 60's.

NEW MONEY BUY

A stock deemed particularly appropriate for the nouveau riche investor, often resulting in particularly heavy trading in the Dallas and Beverly Hills offices.

NEW SOUTH, THE

Fast growing part of the Sunbelt best epitomized by a BMW with a gun rack.

THE NEWS FROM ABROAD

Barbara Walters' specials.

NEWARK

A prototype of where the American city is going.

NEWS

A rumor the trader just heard.

OLD NEWS

A rumor the trader heard ten minutes ago.

LORE

Something that has been picked up by the media.

NIGHT OF THE LIVING DEAD

The annual partnership dinner-dance at Lazard Freres.

NINETY-SIX IN THE SHADE

An apt description of the construction crew on a typical August morning on the Long Island Expressway.

NON-RECURRING FACTORS

One-time events that management could not be expected to have anticipated, e.g. a downturn in the business cycle, price competition, or a rise in the cost of raw materials.

NO BRAINER

An investment seemingly without risk, and usually one without reward except to whoever pointed it out to you.

NOBLESSE OBLIGE

Cultured, responsible behavior exhibited in decreasing quantities by Old Money, New Money, Lottery Winners, and Internet Entrepreneurs.

NON-COMPETE CLAUSE

A contract stipulation clearly not ever entered into by Pete Rose.

NORMAL PORTFOLIO

What a naive person with no particular skill (e.g. a consultant) might choose to buy if he were randomly building a portfolio. (See Benchmark.)

NORTH OF BATON ROUGE

The upper boundary beyond which, it is said, no attractive oil deal ever gets.

NOTRE DAME

A football team that amazingly, year after year, fields an above-average university.

NUMBER, THE

Individually derived financial objective that would allow one to live comfortably from his conservatively invested capital. The Number is higher for those with expensive tastes or an ex-wife. There is no Number for those with two or more ex-wives.

O

OENOPHILE

Anyone who owns more than one corkscrew.

"O.J. WAS INNOCENT"

Soon to be a major motion picture by Oliver Stone.

OKLAHOMA

A state which, some say, will never have a professional football team because then Texas would want one too.

ONE DECISION STOCKS

Stocks that reputedly can be bought and put away forever. (See Unicorn.)

ONE HOUR ON THE STAIRMASTER AT 6 A.M.

The thought most likely to cause a bond trader to go back to sleep. (See Turnover.)

ONE INVESTOR AT A TIME

A slow but effective way eventually to screw all the investors.

ONE TOKE OVER THE LINE

How money managers relaxed in the '60's.

ONE TRICK PONY

Money manager so devoid of creativity that his investment style actually matches that described in his firm's brochure.

OPEN OUTCRY

What can be heard as the result of a margin call.

ORAL CONTRACT

- ❖ An agreement said not to be worth the paper it's written on.
- ❖ A professor's promise of tenure at a religious college in Tulsa, Oklahoma.
- ❖ What actress Linda Lovelace had with her producer.

❖   In today's legal slang, a "Lewinsky."

ORGANIZATION CHART

Schematic representation of reporting relationships carefully observed by poorly managed companies.

ORGANIZED LABOR

What unionism used to be.

ORIGINAL ART, YACHTS, AND GULFSTREAM JETS

The second, third, and fourth best ways to spend really big money fast.

"OTHER INCOME"

An item in the financial statements which should be viewed with skepticism, along with Revenues, Cost of Goods Sold, SG and A and the entire balance sheet.

OUT OF THE MONEY OPTIONS

Puts or calls entailing significant risk for the investor, as are in the money and at the money options.

OUT THE WINDOW

Where the syndicate manager is after an unsuccessful offering.

OUT TO LUNCH

Where your broker usually is if you need anything other than to place an order.

OUTSOURCING

Recent trend in business whereby routine activities are contracted out to specialists so that corporate managers can concentrate on running the business. Managers' favorite activities to outsource include payroll, printing, pension management, and parenthood.

OVEREXTENDED

Dolly Parton's tee shirt.

OVERHEAD SUPPLY

Where the stews hide the pillows on long tourist flights.

OVERNIGHT POSITION

A position taken by a block trader which he hopes to maintain comfortably for the entire night. Not to be confused with the missionary position.

OVERPRICED

A seemingly perennial condition of good technology stocks and single malt Scotch.

OXYMORON

- ❖ Massachusetts Republican.
- ❖ Punk rock.

P

Painting the Tape

Intentional sloppy buying in an issue with the intent of attracting other potential buyers at hopefully even higher prices. The practice is largely limited to very young managers of other people's money.

Palm Beach

A city populated by old money with new money aspirations.

Palm Springs

Where Los Angelenos go to do what they do in LA, except with greater hassle and expense.

Paper Portfolio Manager

One who plays the financial equivalent of air guitar.

Paper Trail

A thoroughfare littered with forms, memos, and letters, usually prepared hastily after the fact to provide evidence that something did or didn't happen. (See CYA, or Cover Your Anatomy.)

Par

1000 in the bond market, 100 in the stock market, and 39 with mulligans on the front nine.

Paris

The city of lightweight investment firms but good currency traders. Natives hold Americans in the same high regard as they formerly reserved for the Brits.

Park Avenue

A thoroughfare upon which short sellers once did not own homes.

Pass Don't-Pass Line

The check-in counter at Caesar's Palace the night of the big fight.

Pencil Neck Geek

A socially inept individual who inexplicably gains charisma and grace when your P.C. goes down.

PENNY STOCK

A security which was once a dollar stock.

PEOPLE SKILLS

The ability to quickly make the right friends and enemies.

PERFORMANCE FEE

Good reason to fire your manager if it improves his performance.

PERFORMANCE MEASUREMENT

The art and/or science of so selecting the portfolios, the measurement period, or the benchmark in a way that one can legitimately claim top quartile numbers.

PERMANENTLY HIGH PLATEAU

- ❖ Where the experts will almost certainly again say stocks are trading just before the next protracted bear market begins.
- ❖ What stocks will have reached just about the time O.J. finds the real killer.

PERPETUITY

- ❖ Seemingly, the time taken to play eighteen holes on Ladies' Day.
- ❖ Two days in Davenport.
- ❖ A research meeting on Friday afternoon.

PERSONAL TRAINER

A professional athlete whose expertise is enlisted to provide technical advice and encouragement, kind of like an investment advisor without discretion.

PHARMACEUTICALS

An industry which represents 7% of the cost of health care and gets 90% of the blame for escalating health care costs.

PHILADELPHIA

Home of the Philadelphia Stock Exchange, and a place W. C. Fields would rather be than where he is now.

PHILATELY

Investment in collectibles once favored by Ways and Means chairman Rostenkowski.

PHOENIX

❖ In Roman mythology, a stock that rises from the ashes of Chapter 11 bankruptcy and, with tighter cost controls and ever diminishing debt, regains Wall Street favor and again flies high. (See Icarus.)

❖ A city in Arizona where wealthy Sedonans go in winter.

PHYSICAL FITNESS

A level of conditioning requiring such an expenditure of time that it can be attained only by the top and bottom 5% of the firm.

PIGTAIL

An eccentrism usually affected only by those utterly immune to social convention, e.g. merchant seamen, grade school girls, and derivatives experts.

PILGRIM

❖ A beginning investor, particularly in speculative issues such as commodities and derivatives.

❖ Casual acquaintance of John Wayne.

PINK SHEETS

What San Francisco stock brokers sleep on.

PLAGIARISM

A form of research that utilizes only one source.

PLAYING HURT

The willingness to show up and take care of business even when sick, hung over, or undergoing an I.R.S. audit.

PLUGGED AND ABANDONED

❖ A term applied to any oil wells that the drilling fund operator no longer considers a hot prospect

❖ The fate, apparently, of most individuals recruited by the Arkansas Highway Patrol.

POCKETS OF OPPORTUNITY

What light-fingered malcreants often pick in the Wall Street area during rush hour. It is alleged that pockets are also picked on the exchange floor and occasionally by upstairs traders.

POLITICAL CORRECTNESS

A particularly invidious form of bigotry, in which the perpetrator's obsession with race, sex, and religion is disguised as concern for minority sensibilities.

POLO LOUNGE

Once and future place to see fathers with their daughters, hear about hot media stocks, and air out your ponies.

PONZI, CHARLES

First quartile performer for a time in the 20's, with an eclectic investment style and a flair for marketing, which is said to have made him beloved of the era's consultants.

"POPULAR DELUSIONS AND THE MADNESS OF CROWDS"

- ❖ Famous sociological study of mass hysteria which traces its tendency to inflate prices to ridiculous extremes, e.g. tulips, the South Sea Bubble, and Internet retailers.

- ❖ The presidential candidacy of Ross Perot.

POROSITY

An inexact measure of just how full of holes the drilling fund operator's story really is.

PORSCHE 911 WHALETAIL TURBO

A sports car which inexplicably seems to cause its owner to grow a paunch and a little bald spot.

PORT

- ❖ The location from which goods enter or leave the country.

- ❖ What you are facing on the senior partner's yacht when the pointy end is on your right and the round end is on your left, unless you are romantically involved with someone, in which case the directions may have to be reversed.

PORTFOLIO INSURANCE

Means of insuring that upside performance will be limited, and that downside performance may be reduced.

PORTFOLIO MANAGER

The place where the buck stops (always) and the bucks stop (in good years).

PORTFOLIO STRATEGIST

The person in the research department responsible for making the analyst's recommendations relate in some way to the firm's economic outlook and to each other without antagonizing the firm's banking clients or embarrassing its asset management department.

POST

❖ The physical place on the exchange floor where a particular issue is traded by a specialist.

❖ What some disgruntled investors say that some specialists are as dumb as.

❖ The word from which the term "going postal" is derived.

PREANNOUNCE

The increasingly frequent tendency of companies to alert the Street to an earnings shortfall and relatedly the tendency of portfolio managers to enumerate, in great detail, prior to a golf match, all of their various afflictions and infirmities.

PREDICTABLE CORPORATE REACTIONS

In response to any new idea,

❖ The Marketing Department will be for it.

❖ Finance will be against it.

❖ Human Resources will view it with alarm.

❖ The EDP Department will need more memory.

PRENUP (OR PRENUPTIAL AGREEMENT)

A kind of letter of intent, non-binding on either party and often invalidated by subsequent events, which is nevertheless of critical importance in allowing the divorce lawyer to extract a fee even if there is no divorce. (See Portfolio Insurance.)

PRESIDENT CLINTON'S SHORT LIST

Robert Reich, Donna Shalala, and foreign policy accomplishments during the first term.

PRICE

A fundamental factor….. the only thing you know for sure about a stock.

PRICE WAR

- ❖ Something very good for consumers but very bad for your portfolio. Price wars get worse and last longer than analysts think they will.

- ❖ Probably what General Sherman had in mind when he said "War is Hell."

PRIMA DONNA

Anyone in the investment business whose last two decisions have been right.

PRIME RATE

That rate of interest charged by banks to their most important customers, i.e. those with whom they conduct other, high-margin, non-lending business.

PRIMROSE

A path down which many an unsuspecting investor has trod. Can be used as a verb. Eq. Goldman has primrosed the trust departments again.

PRINCESS

An oversized tennis racquet popular in San Francisco.

PRINCETON

Hands down, the Ivy with the best approach to improving legal education in America.

PRIVATE PLACEMENT

Careful arrangement of one's athletic supporter during a match.

PRODUCER

Retail broker who, utilizing his firm's research, executive capabilities, office space, and reputation, single-handedly produces commissions. Producers are highly sought because of their almost legendary loyalty to the firms which employ them.

PROFESSIONAL SOCIETY

An association of like-minded people designed to limit new entrants, reduce capacity, and prevent price competition so they can become more like the real professions of law and medicine.

PROGRAM TRADE

An informationless trade where the trader is aware that he doesn't have information.

PROSPECTUS

A long, involved and arcane document which is written by the lowest paid quartile in the investment banker's firm and read only by the lowest paid quartile at the SEC.

PROSPECTUS, FRIENDLY

As above, but with pictures.

PROXY VOTING

A process whereby rank-and-file shareholders get to vote on major matters of corporate governance, such as selection of company auditors.

PRUDENT MAN RULE

❖ The basic law governing the actions of fiduciaries, providing that they must act as would a prudent man minding his own affairs or those of his mother-in-law.

❖ The dictum suggesting discretion and ambiguity when asked for a subjective opinion by a female acquaintance.

Q

Qualified Statement

Something you are definitely not qualified to deal with.

Quality of Earnings

An attribute highly sought after and revered during bear markets.

Quality of Management

An attribute which security analysts are particularly adept at assessing, in spite of their narrow frame of reference, very brief exposure to said management, and almost total lack of experience in an industrial environment.

Quant

A particular type of security analyst who would rather be precisely wrong than generally right.

Quartile

One fourth of the full universe of results. Amazingly, all U.S. money managers are in the top quartile of investment performance.

R

R & D

Research and Development

- ❖ A pit into which management pours money in hopes of an occasional Eureka.
- ❖ A corporate department known for producing cures for which there is no known disease.

Railroad

Two streaks of rust and a growing deficit.

Random Walk

An academic theorem which holds that managerial competence is a non-recurring factor. The theorem is silent, however, on managerial incompetence.

Rap Account

Da broka 2 da boyz
Da fee B 3
U pay no commission
But da fee B 3.

Real Rate of Return

That amount of money left over from a profitable stock transaction after brokerage, taxes, and your wife has redecorated the living room.

Realized Gain

The only kind of gain there is. Computing unrealized "gains" is like splitting up the loot before robbing the train.

Reboot

What John Wayne did every morning.

Recession

An economic downturn usually signaled by your neighbor losing his job.

DEPRESSION

When you lose your job.

PANIC

When your wife loses her job.

RECOMMENDED LIST

A roster of stocks that the brokerage firm's investment committee would presumably buy if their investment objectives were what they presume their clients' objectives to be.

RED HERRING

A preliminary prospectus, the front page of which is printed in red. Differs from the final prospectus primarily in that it clearly states that it is preliminary and incomplete.

REIT

A stock which behaves like the underlying real estate during uptrends in the stock market, and like a common stock during market declines.

RELATIVE RETURN

- ❖ What plan sponsors demand in bull markets while absolute return is stressed in bear phases.
- ❖ The supposed killing your brother-in-law just made.

REPO

What can happen to the Porsche of a bond trader too long wrong.

RESEARCH

A type of plagiarism utilizing more than one source.

RESEARCH CALL

Early morning session on the squawk box which allows the analyst the chance to defend his recommendations and the broker a chance to read the morning paper.

RESEARCH MEETING

An event, usually held weekly, at which security analysts explain to portfolio managers why they have reduced their earnings estimates.

RESERVES

An estimate of the barrels of oil or natural gas equivalents that an oil company owns. "Proven" reserves are the result of a well actually having been drilled in the area, with hopefully valid extrapolations made for the full field. "Unproven" reserves are based on the seismic and/or astrological work of other Texans from outside the company.

REVENUE BOND

A security which produces substantial revenue for fast-talking muni salesmen.

RISK-ADJUSTED PERFORMANCE

What your golf score would be without sand traps, woods, and water.

RISK AVERSION

A psychosis resulting in one's tendency to buy electric utility stocks and drive with the air bag inflated.

RISK FACTORS

- ❖ Drawing to an inside straight.
- ❖ Knocking late with nine or ten.
- ❖ Playing the new issue market.

RISKLESS TRANSACTION

See Hillary Trade.

RETIREMENT

A status devoutly sought by many employees who, unless they are airline pilots or postal workers, would then greatly reduce their average weekly hours worked.

ROAD RAGE

What you get on the third day of a five-day business trip.

ROCKET SCIENTIST

A designer of sophisticated derivative versions of "heads I win, tails you lose" propositions.

ROLE MODEL

Any athlete, rock star, or other celebrity who earns a good living without doing anything unpleasant.

ROLEX

An unsubtle timepiece, more favored by bean traders than compliance officers, by Texans than Vermonters, and by bulls than bears.

R.R.

A Roll Royce in Beverly Hills, a Range Rover in Greenwich, and a Rolling Rock in Latrobe.

ROOKIE MISTAKE

The tendency for young institutional salesmen to talk with the monkey instead of the organ grinder.

ROSE AMONG THORNS

Maria Bartoromo, live from the floor of the New York Stock Exchange.

RULE FOR ACQUIRING TOYS

"If it floats, flies or fellates, lease it."

S

Santa Fe

Only state capital without commercial air service, and only state pension fund with its own helipad. (See Harmonic Convergence and Blue Corn Tacos.)

Santa Monica Freeway

An elongated parking lot in Southern California. Said to be least crowded at 10 a.m. on Sundays, when the Protestants are in church, the Jews are in Palm Springs, and the Catholics are trying to get their cars started.

Saucy, Slightly Fruity, with a Pert Insouciance

The owner of a successful wine bar near North Beach.

Scarsdale Fats

- ❖ An upstart tennis league set to challenge the Virginia Slims.
- ❖ Foods to avoid when visiting Westchester County.

Scorched Earth

The ground beneath a Tina Turner concert.

Scores

- ❖ Derivative issue representing a basket of securities.
- ❖ What the bachelor bond trader does a lot less often than he says.
- ❖ Purchases or acquires, as tickets to a Grateful Dead Concert.

Seasonal Adjustment

- ❖ Statistical technique for forecasting annual sales of Panama hats based on sales data for February.
- ❖ Minor alteration in the recipes at Szechuan House on Ladies' Day.

Seattle

City of green trees and white sailboats nestled between the Puget Sound and majestic Mount Olympus. Home to grunge rock, café latte, and gateway to Redmond. Increasingly known for high tech companies in what is called the Silicon Rainforest, so named because the rainy season lasts from October to September.

SEC

An effective and very inexpensive training ground for member firm compliance officers. As an enforcement agency, said to be about as effective as the chaperone at a high school dance.

SECTOR ROTATOR

One who buys into a group once its upside potential has been exhausted.

SECULAR BULL MARKET

An uptrend expected to last beyond the current options expirations.

SECURITY ANALYST

A professional whose primary function is to explain why a stock is priced where it is, which most of them do exceedingly well. Those who attempt to forecast, however, do so at extreme peril to themselves and their profession.

SELL SIGNAL

- ❖ When the company announces a new corporate headquarters.
- ❖ When the CEO puts the conference call on hold.
- ❖ When the stock runs off the top (or bottom) of the chart.

75 AND 3 OVER

Age distribution of the average foursome at a Fort Lauderdale country club.

SEXUAL HARASSMENT LITIGATION

A lawsuit probably not initiated by Xena, Warrior Princess.

SHABBY GENTILITY

A lifestyle of frugal intellectualism affected by some academics east of the San Gabriel Mountains.

SHADES OF GRAY

Prescription sun glasses often affected by Hollywood moguls to color-coordinate with their silver hair and charcoal turtlenecks.

SHELL GAME

A contest involving neither skill nor luck. (See Day Trading.)

SHORT ACRE

Real estatese for a parcel measuring 50 feet by 100.

SHORT SELLER

A broker from Nomura Securities.

SHORT SQUEEZE

The best girlfriend of a broker from Nomura Securities.

SILICON VALLEY, THE

Cleavage often visible at formal Bay Area affairs.

SIX INCHES ON THE GROUND AND NEW POWDER

Lorena Bobbit's idea of a perfect ski vacation.

SKULL AND BONES

A secret society whose current membership reputedly includes Calista Flockhart.

SLANT DRILLING

Stealing ideas from the oil analyst at a competing firm.

SLEEPING WITH THE PRESIDENT

Attending an afternoon White House briefing during the Reagan years.

SLICE AND DICE

- ❖ Entertainment industry slang for particularly gory horror films.
- ❖ Investment industry slang for the construction of derivative "products" almost certain to result in particularly gory losses. (See Cosmic Waste.)

SMALL CAP

A form of headgear fancied by hackers and Generation X brokers, almost invariably worn backward.

LARGE CAP

Vividly colored headgear seen in profusion at Salomon Brothers golf outings.

SMALL FORTUNE

What is typically left of a large fortune after a few years trading commodity futures.

THE SMELL OF NAPALM IN THE MORNING

Something every good soldier and every good portfolio manager relishes.

SMOKELESS TOBACCO

Product endorsement opportunity for members of NASCAR, the WWF, and the LPGA.

SNAIL MAIL

Term of derogation, and an insult to gastropods everywhere.

SOBRIETY

The great inhibitor, according to Winston Churchill. Along with chastity, what he asked God to help him obtain but not yet.

SOCIAL STATUS

Condition which increases proportionally to the amount of money you have made, and exponentially with the amount of money you have inherited.

SPANDEX

Synthetic material which has contributed greatly to the principle of truth in packaging.

SPECULATION

Any investment made in the hope of gain. A rank speculation is an investment owned by one's competitor.

SPIKE

The first, low volume high reached by an issue after an extended run, often caused by panicky short covering. If it leads to still further highs, it was not a spike at all, but a breakout.

SPIN CONTROL

Public relations, or the art of perfidious plausible prevention done in a lawyerly manner.

SPLIT

❖ The financial equivalent of getting five nickels for a quarter

❖ A maneuver rarely attempted these days by the Godfather of Soul, James Brown.

❖ What would probably happen to the trousers of James Brown if he did attempt such a maneuver.

REVERSE SPLIT

The financial equivalent of getting a quarter for five nickels.

SQUARE HEADLIGHTS

Another vanishing symbol of engineering excellence in Detroit.

STAGGERED BOARD

Directors who have participated too freely in the post-meeting cocktail party.

STAMPEDE

Unanimous movement in one direction by a large number of organisms, such as cattle or chartists.

STANDSTILL AGREEMENT

Type of contract clearly not entered into by Tina Turner.

STANFORD

The Mother Church of the Silicon Valley, and the place to hire technogeeks with personality.

STAREDOWN

The period during a new account competition when the opposing firms meet in the client's lobby.

STATISTICAL ANALYSIS

An investment technique based on highly quantitative but sometimes misleading data, e.g. the first seven kings of England named Henry had an average of 1.3 wives.

STEERAGE

The way the very rich and the very poor travel.

STIFF COMPETITION

What Pfizer may get from new products for impotence.

STOCK AHEAD

Said of orders that arrived before yours. Wall Street tradition holds that a broker may refuse his client's direction to insert his latest IPO offering in a body orifice on the grounds that there's "stock ahead."

STOCK PICKER

Anyone whose last two selections have worked out.

STONEWALL

A refusal to comment by Messrs. Jagger and Richards regarding the band's smoking habits.

STOP-LOSS

A trading technique highly profitable to writers of market letters and other fiction. When utilized by real life investors, however, it becomes a market order during market routs and may insure that the investor sells at the bottom.

STRIPS, STRAPS, AND STRADDLES

Fun and games at Heidi Fleiss'. (See Golden Handcuffs.)

STRONG HOLD

What your broker calls a stock selling 20% below where he called it a strong buy.

SUBCOMMITTEE

A smaller group thought to be more flexible and responsive than the full committee. If committees tend to design a horse that looks like a camel, a subcommittee can design a horse that looks like an aardvark.

SUMMER RALLY

Any upward move by stocks, no matter how slight, occurring any time between March and November. Widely forecast by market analysts, its eventual occurrence is often cited by them as evidence of their acumen. It is sometimes sufficient in power and scope to offset the declines immediately preceding and following it.

Sun Belt

A wide western belt with the owner's Christian name embroidered on the back. Said to aid cowboys in identifying themselves when they remove their heads from their posteriors.

Sunset Provision

A provision just north of Santa Monica on the San Diego Freeway.

Sun Valley

Great place to shop for outdoor fashions, ski jewelry, and media conglomerates.

Superpatriot

One who doffs his hat when hearing the Jimi Hendrix version of the "Star Spangled Banner."

Supervisory Analyst

A member of the Research Department responsible for editing the written reports of other analysts. Some are single-handedly capable of turning a butterfly into a caterpillar.

Support

❖ A price on a chart which a stock will either go through, reach and stop going down, or not reach at all.

❖ An item of athletic apparel worn by technicians.

Sure Thing

An investment too risky for most investors, and one that should be entered into only by those who can afford the loss.

Surgical Precision

That to which Cher Bono owes her eternal youth.

Surtax

A permanent levy made more palatable by the illusion that it is temporary.

SURVIVAL OF THE FITTEST

Central tenant of capitalism and primary rule at Harry's Bar on a busy night.

SUV

Powerful vehicle with high clearance and four-wheel drive used primarily to transport 110-pound women to the mall.

SWAPS

Winner of the Triple Crown in 1947; the last instance of profitability for this technique.

SWEETHEART DEAL

A nefarious business arrangement which involves giving preferential treatment to a particular customer or client. So called because both parties get kissed, and quite often at least one party gets screwed.

SWITCH

A transaction where the investor may be wrong twice and the broker will be right twice.

T

Tails

❖ The very long-lived liabilities that some insurance policies incur.

❖ What most former "names" at Lloyds of London would like to kick.

Take or Pay Contract

An agreement that, since WHOOPS, no longer gives the bondholder the illusion that his security has some backing.

Take Two Aspirin and Call Me in the Morning

Emergency room procedure for extreme trauma if Hillary's program had passed.

Takeout

A term used in real estate finance. Specifically, it is the kind of food eaten by a developer while trying to refinance his construction loan.

Takeover Candidate

A company which has absolutely no appeal to the buyer of 100 shares, but is presumably very attractive to a buyer of the whole company.

Tape Watcher

A money manager too busy to read research and too timid to call clients.

Tar Heel

What God must be, or the sky wouldn't be Carolina Blue.

Tasteless Drivel, But the Public Will Like It

❖ Vincent Canby reviews a typical Roger Corman film.

❖ The Early Bird Special in Boca Raton.

Tax Code

A document written, seemingly, by the same people who write incentive fee agreements.

TAX-FREE MUNICIPALS

Debentures issued by cities, states, etc. which are free of federal tax, available quotes, and regulation of any kind.

TAX REFORM

A tax increase.

TAX SELLING

An explanation for any price move occurring between the end of September and January. (See Portfolio Dressing, which explains price moves during the other eight months.)

TAX SIMPLIFICATION

An inevitably confusing change in the tax code which makes it impossible for non-professionals to ever figure out how to prepare a return.

TAXATION

According to Lord Keynes, the process of plucking the goose so as to obtain the maximum quantity of feathers with the minimum amount of hissing.

TAXICAB

Public conveyance readily available on pleasant days.

TEAM DECISION-MAKING

A technique utilized by management companies with high personnel turnover so as to save money on reprinting the brochure.

TECHNICAL RALLY

Any uptrend in prices that you don't like or didn't predict.

TECHNICIAN

One who told you so.

TECHNOLOGY STOCKS

The industry group that has produced more capital gains and margin calls than any other.

TEMPORARY ABERRATION

An all-purpose explanation for why the market is going against your most recent (and widely publicized) forecast.

TEN BAGGER

- ❖ Someone extremely unattractive to the opposite sex.

- ❖ Reportedly, Peter Lynch's nickname in high school.

- ❖ A baseball groupie so homely that the whole team wears a bag over their heads in case hers breaks.

10-K

A document filed annually with the SEC listing all of the ten kilometer races that the firm's younger and duller partners have entered.

10-Q

A quarterly version of the same.

10-4

Broderick Crawford saying goodnight to Mrs. C.

TENDER

Said of the sirloin at Christ Cella.

LEGAL TENDER

What you will need plenty of at Christ Cella's.

TERMINAL SHORT

Any company in a regulated industry.

TERRORIST

One with whom, unlike a wife or girlfriend, it is sometimes possible to negotiate.

TEXAS CHAIN SAW MASSACRE, THE

What would happen if Al Dunlap became CEO of Texas Instruments.

"*Thank you, Paine Webber*"

One of two similar-sounding but very different sentiments sometimes expressed to the brokerage and the horse it rode in on.

"*They Aren't Making Any More of It*"

What Mark Twain is said to have said about investment judgment.

13-D

A government document which requires a would-be acquirer to announce that he is acquiring shares for general investment purposes only.

Three Pack-A-Day-Habit

Reportedly, Jack Kennedy's condom usage.

Three Steps and Stumble Rule

A characteristic gait often noticed in those leaving Oscar's after 7:30 p.m.

Thrift Institution

A savings association paying such a low passbook rate that its depositors must live in a very thrifty manner indeed.

Thrifts

❖ Financial institutions which encourage their depositors to be thrifty by paying them very low rates of interest on deposits while charging them very high rates on the few home loans that they make.

❖ A means of transferring wealth from taxpayers to well-connected insiders via government guarantees.

Thundering Herd, The

What can be seen and heard around the main exit from Merrill Lynch headquarters at about two minutes after the close.

Tip

What one may give to or get from a food service employee late in a bull market.

TOE RING

An article of jewelry rarely worn by female security analysts.

TOMBSTONE

A simple advertisement listing the issue in which the firm most recently buried its clients.

TOP DOWN INVESTING

- ❖ An investment approach whereby the manager attempts to construct a whole chicken from a bowl of soup.

- ❖ An approach sometimes pursued by female analysts on Mykinos and Saint Bart's.

- ❖ A style often utilized in Southern California, whereby trades are made by cell phone on the freeway, from a convertible.

TOPLESS IN SEATTLE

Madonna reprises the Meg Ryan role in a planned sequel to the prior hit movie.

TQM

An acronym for Totally Quirky Management, the latest rage among corporate bureaucrats. Proceeds from the premise that one need not have a clue about what he's doing as long as he can identify someone who does and emulate them.

TRACKING ERROR

- ❖ Deviation of an indexed portfolio from its index.

- ❖ A wife's miscalculation in assuming her husband is on the golf course when he is in fact at the marina.

TRADABLE RALLY

A short uptrend, often anticipated by brokers, in a generally declining market, which would theoretically allow one with perfect foresight getting in and perfect foresight getting out to pay both commissions and still not lose money.

TRADING BUY

A particularly attractive investment opportunity in that it produces two commissions.

TRADING HALT

- ❖ Cessation of trading in an issue, pending an announcement. The investor can determine whether the news will be good or bad by noticing whether the stock had been strong or weak prior to the halt. This method has never failed.

- ❖ Something even worse than limit down.

TRANSPORTS, THE

Companies with high labor and energy costs, subject to rigorous regulation and required to operate unprofitable routes on occasion for the public good, are inexplicably recommended for widows, orphans and trust departments.

TREACLE

A research report on one of the firm's investment banking clients.

TREE HUGGER

A psychopathic environmentalist, who would impede industrial progress for the sake of a few birds and bunnies. Often professes love of the great outdoors even though he doesn't read *Field and Stream*.

TREND

Any favorable occurrence in Wall Street that happens twice. A favorable occurrence happening three times is immediately labeled a tradition. Unfavorable developments, no matter how often they occur, are called aberrations.

TREND FOLLOWER

- ❖ Buying whatever is popular at the moment. Akin to betting the favorite to show.

- ❖ One who is long at the top, short at the bottom, and proud of it.

- ❖ A restauranteur who is still waiting to see if pizza is a fad.

TREND SETTER

One whose closet includes both a leisure suit *and* a Nehru jacket.

TRICKLE DOWN ECONOMICS

The economic thesis which holds that the best way to feed grain to the chickens is first to run it through the cow.

TRILATERAL COMMISSION

A secret international cabal thought by some to control interest rates, stock prices, and weekend weather.

TRIPLE NET

What you have fallen into when you fail to nail down expense stops.

TRIPLE WITCHING

When both of your wife's sisters visit you at once.

TRIPLE WITCHING HOUR

Those thankfully rare occasions when your wife, her sister, and your mother-in-law are required by circumstances to be together.

TROPHY PROPERTY

A piece of real estate which provides prestige and pride of ownership in lieu of cash flow. (A trophy wife is said to provide neither.)

TRUST DEPARTMENT

Is to commercial banking as "equities in Dallas" is to Salomon Brothers.

TRUTH IN LENDING

The loan shark's assertion that his rates are comparable to those of major credit card issuers.

TRUTH IN LENDING LAW

Legislation that resulted in a fivefold increase in the numbers of words describing the loan agreement, and a fivefold decrease in the size of the type and the comprehension thereof.

TUBULAR

What West Coast traders call a three-to-one up day on heavy volume.

TWELVE YEAR OLD, SCOTCH

The kind of boy most likely to be invited to Michael Jackson's new place outside Edinburgh.

"21"

A former speakeasy now favored by investment bankers when spending the client's money. Derives its name from the dollar price of its off-the-menu cheeseburger.

TWO HOURS FROM THE DENVER AIRPORT

Where you may well be stuck on Interstate 70 about half way to your new condo in Beaver Creek.

U

ULTIMATE TRUTH

"All Growth is Temporary."

UNDERWRITING SPREAD

Whatever is on the butter tray in the Morgan Stanley dining room.

UNICORN

A mythical beast with one horn. (See Customer's Yachts and Riskless Transaction.)

UNIFORM GIFTS TO MINORS ACT

Since the Tax Reform Act of 1986, a means of making a tax-free distribution to a minor child of one's old uniforms and used clothing.

U.S. POSTAL SERVICE

❖ A welfare system operated by the Federal Government, soon to be rendered obsolete by fax machines, computer networks, UPS and FedEx.

❖ What health care will look like if the government takes it over.

UNREALIZED GAIN

An oxymoron, like riskless transaction and passive management. A gain does not exist until the stock is sold and the check clears.

UPTOWN

❖ Interim stop for money management home offices leaving Wall Street and heading inevitably for Connecticut.

❖ Description of the mode of dress for an institutional salesman on the weekend.

USURY

A limitation on the rate of interest that can be charged by any entity other than the IRS.

UTILITIES

A class of stocks which allow one to lose money at a slower rate in a bear market.

V

VALUATION

Reason often cited for stocks being either "too high" or "too low," often by different people at the same time.

VANISHING FAMILY FARMER

One of the major reasons for the rising standard of living in the Farm Belt and elsewhere.

VARIABLE COSTS

Costs of production which vary with production when volume is increasing, but remain fixed when volume declines.

VEGETARIAN

A Korean who owns a dog.

VELCRO FLY

A device facilitating time-efficient foreplay, said to be favored by some Little Rock tailors.

VELOCITY

A technical economic term which describes, but does not measure, the turnover of money. Economists blame velocity when their forecasts are in error.

VENTURE CAPITAL FUND

A partnership in which the general partner contributes experience and the limited partners contribute the money. At the end of the ten-year life of the fund, the general partner has the money and the limiteds have the experience.

VESTING

A mode of dress sometimes adopted by those with a rack full of gravy-stained Hermes.

VILLAGE PEOPLE, THE

Wall Streeters with very short commutes.

Vintage Furnishings and the Unmistakable Smell of Cigar-Smoked Leather

Description of a typical member of the Union League Club.

Volatility

A characteristic of markets much to be desired during rising trends.

.

W

Wakeup Call

What comes awfully early for traders on the West Coast.

Wall Street

A one-way thoroughfare, with a river at one end and a graveyard at the other, where one can buy contraband drugs by day and investment advice by night, or vice versa.

Wall Street Etiquette (Fishing)

One feigns some degree of interest in his fishing partner's scrawny catch, and does not allude to the purely fortuitous factors which led to it.

Wall Street Etiquette (General)

One is never unintentionally rude.

Wall Street Etiquette (Gin Rummy)

One drums his fingers only lightly when deciding what to discard.

Wall Street Etiquette (Golf)

One does not intentionally step on his opponents lost ball while deciding whether to announce it "found."

Wall Street Etiquette (Poker)

One occasionally antes without being asked.

Wall Street Etiquette (Sailing)

One allows, under non-race conditions of course, the burdened vessel to leeward to enter the harbor ahead of him, unless his own crew is either cold, wet, or tired.

Wall Street Etiquette (Social)

One always calls the morning after even if he has no intention of ever calling again.

Wall Street Etiquette (Tennis)

One is very careful to make generally plausible line calls.

WALL STREET WEEK

On average, 3-1/2 days.

WAL-MART

Well managed retailer offering merchandise ranging from upscale mobile home furnishings to men's wash and wear business suits.

WASHBOARD ABS

What you may well need if incarcerated for laundering money.

WASHINGTON

A city of Northern charm and Southern efficiency.

WASHINGTON, GEORGE; LINCOLN, ABRAHAM; AND BROWN, RON

Three politicians who have their face on the side of a mountain.

WATCHDOG

An outside director expected to protect the interest of the common shareholder even though he is selected, retained, paid, and has his parking validated by management.

WEATHER

A factor which seems to have particularly negative influence on the earnings of weak, poorly managed second-tier firms.

WEB SITE

Often, a dusty spidery area atop the lawyer's Pro Bono file.

WEST OF SEPULVEDA

❖   The low-smog area of Los Angeles.

❖   That area of Los Angeles where it is hardest to see the air.

❖   A two-three block sliver said to contain all intelligent life in Los Angeles.

WHIPSAW

When you buy an electric utility up a quarter and immediately see it decline an eighth.

WHISPER NUMBER

A telephone number sometimes dialed by bond traders during market lulls
1-900-HOTSEXX.

WHITE KNIGHT

Quite often, a term applied to the least effective jumper on an NBA team.

WHITE SHOE

Often said of a firm somewhat weak in the areas of research, sales, trading, and investment banking.

GREEN SHOE

An over-allotment made to a white shoe firm when the deal is really out the window.

WHOOPS

One of the milder exclamations from those whose municipal bonds defaulted.
(See Open Outcry.)

WIDOWMAKER

A slang term sometimes applied to Lookback Options.

WIDOWS AND ORPHANS

A class of investors for whom speculative issues are inappropriate until they have risen substantially.

WINDOW DRESSING

- ❖ Rearranging the portfolio at month, quarter, or year-end to eliminate obvious losers and emphasize recent winners.

- ❖ The receptionist at most Beverly Hills brokerages.

- ❖ That which one puts on his salad at the restaurant atop the World Trade Building.

WIRE

A method whereby a retail firm provides instant analysis of fast breaking events in order to help shape long-term investment policy.

WIRED

- ❖ Holding aces back-to-back in stud poker.
- ❖ In a state of barely controlled excitement.
- ❖ Done in by a retail brokerage or wire house.

WITCH OF WALL STREET

- ❖ Hetty Green.
- ❖ The senior partner's second wife.

WITH SQUARED SHOULDERS AND A MANLY GAIT

The way the golf course is attacked by more than a few members of the LPGA.

WOEFULLY INADEQUATE

- ❖ Management's reaction to a takeover bid at $60 when the prior decade's high for the stock has been $42.
- ❖ Always futile attempts by central banks to prop up their currencies.
- ❖ Capital infusions into sick retail companies.
- ❖ Madonna's last three honeymoon companions.

WOODWORK

An activity for senior citizens sometimes facilitated by Viagra.

WORKOUT

- ❖ Chapter 11 of Jane Fonda's book.
- ❖ A term you don't want to hear applied to one of your venture capital holdings.

WRANGLER

Term used in some Southwestern firms for the guy who manages the secretarial pool.

WRIGLEY FIELD

A friendly confine conveniently located about nine miles from where professional baseball is played.

WRINKLE ROOM

That area of a Miami restaurant where the early bird special is served.

WRITE-OFF

- ❖ A non-recurring factor which occurs about every three years for some companies.

- ❖ A corporate mulligan.

- ❖ What playground kids call a do-over.

X

X Files

Where a broker keeps his customer complaints.

X Rated

- ❖ A bond below the level of Bbb.

- ❖ Motion pictures particularly attractive to people below the age of sixteen.

Xaviera Hollander

Early Wall Street proponent of the butterfly spread.

Xenophobic

Said of a portfolio holding no ADR's.

Xerox

- ❖ Archetypical growth stock of the 60's.

- ❖ Archetypical institutional favorite of the 70's.

- ❖ Archetypical trust department holding of the 80's.

- ❖ Archetypical turnaround of the 90's.

Xero

The price below which Xerox will not trade.

Y

Y Chromosome

Until very recently, one of the requirements for partnership at Goldman.

Y-Shaped Coffin

What Madonna, some say, will be buried in.

Yacht

What you call your sailboat when discussing it with somebody highly unlikely to ever see it.

Yahoo

What one yells on an up day when long on the right Internet stocks.

Yale

Thought of be the best institution of higher learning in New Haven and known to be the alma mater of Montgomery Burns.

Yankee Bonds

- ❖ The 11% long treasuries produced by Jimmy Carter's economic policies.
- ❖ The warm feelings that George Steinbrenner engenders in his players.

Yarborough

What bridge players call a portfolio of penny stocks.

Yawl

- ❖ Fore and aft rigged sailboat favored by Boston money managers for its ease in single-handling.
- ❖ How the Atlanta branch manager addresses the home office.

Yawn

Not a good thing to do during the client's recitation of his routine investment objectives.

Yeoman

A portfolio manager without a press agent.

YIELD

A request often made by bond traders in various singles bars around Manhattan.

YIELD TO MATURITY

Argument by some bond traders for May-December romance.

YOKEL

Someone who lives west of the Hudson River.

YUGO

A bear market Mercedes.

Z

ZAFTIG

Like Karen Carpenter, before interest, taxes, depreciation, and amortization.

ZAG

What you sometimes do when you should zig.

ZEALOT

One who has discovered an approach to the market which is currently working.

ZED

The level below which the Financial Times Index will not decline.

ZEN BUDDHISM

An Eastern religious sect which gave rise to theories involving right-brain, left-brain dichotomies, achieving oneness with the universe, and the Tao Jones Average.

ZERO

❖ The level where downside risk in a stock is least.

❖ The percentage of people who should answer a margin call.

❖ Mean temperature near the lake in Chicago during November through April.

ZERO COUPON BOND

A bond on which the IRS collects income tax even though there is no income.

ZONE

❖ A theoretical state sometimes achieved by an athlete or investor where consciousness is raised, performance is greatly enhanced, and a heightened sense of self confidence ensues.
❖ A lucky streak.

ZOO

Where the margin clerks sit in a wire house.

ZSA ZSA

A slaphappy former jailbird and jewelry recipient.

www.ingramcontent.com/pod-product-compliance
Lightning Source LLC
Chambersburg PA
CBHW080011210526

45170CB00015B/1977

* 9 7 8 0 5 9 5 1 5 5 0 6 4 *